What Am I Called To Be

Ruth Thompson

To order additional copies of this book, contact:
Xlibris
844-714-8691
www.Xlibris.com
Orders@Xlibris.com

ISBN: Softcover   978-1-6641-8136-6
       Hardcover   978-1-6641-8138-0
       EBook   978-1-6641-8137-3

Print information available on the last page

Rev. date: 06/28/2021

Look at Me! Look at ME! It's Ms. Ruth, in action, TIME to TEACH POETRY,

LESSONS to make my STUDENTS feel, as TALL, as a TREE

From all my SPECIAL MOMENTS of POETRY, that has made you all SOAR!

Soon, I'll be on the PLANE, and ready to be on... TOUR!

Hello Everyone, Welcome, to Ms Ruth's world! Full of FUN, ADVENTURE, and JOY for each LIVES, I've TOUCHED as a No 1 TEACHER. 1 way or another, for 26 yrs of teaching, as a Pre-School Teacher, Site Supervisor, for OLDER children, 6-11; and a Private TUTOR, for ALL AGES... up to age 19.

How is that?

This EXPERIENCE has been so REWARDING/ FUFULLING, throughout my TEACHING CAREER!

You will LEARN a lot about DESTINY as I take you though each STUDENT'S JOURNEY....to find their OWN!

This book is DEDICATED to my 2 NEICES, Kayla and Briana, who have been my No 1 INSPIRATION as a WRITER. Kayla and Briana, has EXCELLED to GREATNESS as you will see in PRECIOUS pictures of LIBERTY in every ASPECT of the WORD!

This is also dedicated to my sister, Marion, who is also known as Marie, and my-brother-law, Beris.

My father, Herbert Thompson, who was also a WRITER. I HONOR him as well, and most importantly for my step Mom, Mrs Jesse, who sadly passed on the same day I completed the book. Thank you Mrs Jesse for taking care of my dad Herbert Thompson! The 2 of you are now 1 again....in heaven! RIP

And to my uncle Basil, my dad's brother, who passed 2 days before Mrs Jesse.

Ma Mitchell, I THANK the lord for DESTINY to be KIND to me, for USING your son Tyrone. To BLESS me with a place to STAY with you/family... from that moment in 20002 until now, you have been my No INSPIRATION/CHEERLEADER with your sneakers and pom pom (in SPIRIT) THANK you for TRULY being there for me, Love you much!

And my other mom Mattos! Ma Mattos, I THANK TREVEIL, your daughter, my old HAIR stylist in NJ for allowing me to SHARE you! Love you much! Also Mrs Etlyn Gardner, my sister, Linda's GODMOTHER, who became my GODMOTHER (I stole her, in London). She led me to the lord, and GUIDED me throughout my JOURNEY in life. We called her GODY! A very WISE old W.O.G I miss her! RIP!

And for Mrs Zenifer Khan, another Woman of God who MENTORED me SPIRITUALLY. Her MANTLE lives on with me! Like Elijah and Elisha. RIP grandma!

Cousin Barbara, Mark, Glaister, uncle Casbert's son, and Christine
my sister, Linda, and Michael, with the rest of the family...you will
ENJOY in London, along with Keith, my brother, Rose my big sister,
and Donald... God BLESS you...I Love you all!

I would also love to HONOR my BEST friend Carol, who has been there for me, LIFTING/ ENCOURING me, whenever I NEEDED it…

Dona, who has been there for me, and allowing me to MINISTER in SONG on her Birthday! My friend Shonda, who I've known since 2007, a real DESTINY HELPER! Thanks girl!

To my Coworkers: Lisa, Ms Brown and Ms Stacy, you all were the BEST TEACHERS I could ask for. We ALL had FUN after work. Lisa, THANK you for HONORING me as a GIFTED TEACHER you called me, and typed/printed my POEMS out for my STUDENTS/GIFT for the OUTSTANDING ones like Nicolas, Francis and Jasmin, as you will see as I HONOR them in my book! Mrs Brown, you DEMONSTRATED your GIFT with your SPECIAL NEED Student Noel, who became OUTSTANDING… through you. AWESOME! Ms Stacey, THANK you for ALLOWING your son Maurice, to become part of my book., and always ASKING for me. Mrs Anglia, you were such a BLESSING as we work alongside together as TEACHERS! I THANK you for BLESSING me with my QUEEN CUSHION for my HEAD TEACHER seat.

Miss Ruth's Personal Poetry

My dog Ruffus

My dog Ruffus is
A lot of fun
He's my pet, my
Mommy brought me
And he's always on
the run run run he's
always on the run

MY Little Bunny

My bunny. My bunny

Goes hop hop hop

Hopping so fast I can't make him stop

When I gave him a carrot

He than took

My Cat Micah

My cat Micah is a very special cat

He likes to sit in his Basket

In the kitchen is where it's at

He has green eyes

That sees in the Dark

And he doesn't like to swim

Or see that great shark

Shining Star
I am a shining
star so bright,
look at me I'm
out of sight.

by Miss Ruth

Poem: An Apple a Day!

An apple a day, keeps the dentist away,
go on and crunch, and then you can munch,
A is for apple, that goes up and down and across,
and then they take a floss😄

What COUNTRY do I come from?
I need to ask my mom and DAD.
If I don't know, my parents told me.

I come from Jamaica, Trinidad, India, America, Puerto Rico, and this makes me so... GLAD
No matter WHERE we COME from....there is UNITY.
Most countries have their INDEPENDENCE... which means.... we are FREE!

What kind of HAIR, do I have?
Straight, Curly, Kinky, or Wavy, can be ME.
Very Short, or in-between, maybe very long hair, as tall as a TREE
No matter, how we style or wear it, under our HAT!
Mommy puts rollers in her hair, as we sit on the... MAT

The day I was born, I carried a SPECIAL STAR
A star of GREATNESS, and have love from my parents
who was so excited that I'm finally HERE.
My whole family threw a big party celebration for my BIRTHDAY
Full of laughter ......and CHEER!

The opposite of UP or DOWN,

like at a CIRCUS here comes a CLOWN

He takes off his hat, and the opposite of 'take off is ….ON!

Like a Christmas tree   that has the lights UP!

 The opposite   of LIGHT   is DARK, and like in the blue   sea!...

watch out!

For a… SHARK!

CHILDREN/ PARENTS. ....ENJOY! Also
REMEMBER Ms. Ruth's MOTTO!

Pick up your WINGS! and FLY! like a BEAUTIFUL BUTTERFLY

Thank you!

INTRODUCING ALL Children/Young Adults to the GIFT/ART... of
POETRY, will TEACH them, that they can BECOME ANYTHING in this
world that they WANT to BE! I have also MENTORED STUDENTS, in
GUIDING them to their CAREER GOALS/PROSPECTIVE choices in
life, to EXCEL, them to... SOAR! without... NO limits!

ISIAH

Isiah! Isiah! You are known as ZAY!

Look at you, so handsome as a BABY, and with dimples... what can I SAY!

With all your SPECIAL family gathering AROUND!

For your BABY DEDICATION, you didn't make a SOUND!

Today, your 8 yrs old, loving GYMNASTICS, jumping high on the TRAMPOLINE...

I too enjoyed gymnastics in my day!

I was.... a QUEEN!

NICHOLAS

I have to FIND my STAR of WHAT! I'm SUPOSE to BE,
Flying HIGH, like an EAGLE, SOARING! and being FREE!
Whether a TEACHER, or an ELECTRICIAN, a BAKER, or a MAIL lady
or MAN,
This WILL be quite a JOURNEY for me,
But I KNOW, I WILL be a GOOD brand... Just like then

JAIDEN

Hello! My name is Jaiden, and I know what I want to BECOME,
An ENGINEER! because I love ELECTRONICS of ALL kinds,
I can become an ENTREPRENEUR, and earn a large SUM
My mom SUPPORTS me in my CAREER choice, and this is COOL
1st, she says, I must COMPLETE my work when I'm at....SCHOOL!

NATALIYAH

Dad! dad! WHERE! did the TIME GO!

1 day I was a TODDLER... then I TURNED around like CINDERELLA, all GROWN UP NOW!

As for being a toddler BACK THEN... I say... NO!

TODAY! I am a BUSINESS MINDED, CAREER WOMAN....

all centered around my FAMILY, from my LOVING FATHER, grandmother, uncles, and aunties…

I just gave you a taste of my FAMILY

KAMRIN

Mom! I want to become a TRAVEL NURSE in PSYCHOLOGY,
Caring for the MIND. NURSING them back to HEALTH,
Mentally and Physically, especially when society wants to...GRIND,
I want to TRAVEL, all over the world , and spread my ...LOVE,
My love to become ESTABLISHED/ GRADUATE... and be as sweet
as a DOVE

ARIANNA

Hello! Everyone, my name is Arianna, and I want to become a NURSE,
to attend Nursing School, and EARN a DEGREE,
Caring for YOUNG and OLD,
I just KNOW in my heart that, this is MEANT to BE!
This is the CAREER for ME,
Doing my BEST, and being . .FREE!

JONATHAN

Mom! You know WHAT I want to BECOME, an ARCHAEOLOGIST,
knowing about my American HERITAGE TODAY!
To study DIFFERENT kinds of ROCKS,
like Thomas Jefferson, the 1st man make a BARROW to walk though,
I'm going to EARN my BACHELOR'S DEGREE and then say… .HEY!

😛😄

DARNELL

Darnell! Darnell! Look at YOU.

From age 3 to 9… you've become a good FISHERMAN!… through and THROUGH

WOW! What an excellent hobby, you've chosen, in your spare TIME.

When you were 3 yrs old, with Ms Ruth knew you, SHINING…like a silver DIME

JOSSELYN

Josselyn! Josselyn! Here you ARE!

Look at you, so BEATIFUL like a SHINING STAR!

I am so HONORED and PLEASED to be your TEACHER, 14 years AGO.

The DAY we MET again, at DUNKIN' DONUTS, I am so HAPPY to see you. GROW!

LEA

Lea! Lea! Look at YOU!

MASTERING Ms. Ruth's 1st Christmas POEM though and THROUGH

I'm so PROUD to be your TEACHER. Especially at the Christmas PLAY.

You EARNED your GIFT a SPECIAL doll, because... you made Ms. Ruth's DAY!

ANJALI

Ms Ruth, told me in the '70's, that KUNG FU was GREAT
It PROTECTS you, especially with those HIGH Kicks,
and TODAY! I do KARATE. and it also has a very high RATE.
Those SIDE KICKS are AWESOME, as I kept it up... all this TIME!
One day, I'm going to receive a MEDAL in GOLD!
Also, this will be a cool RHYME.

JAILYN

Princess Jailyn, princess Jailyn!
You look so BEATIFUL, in your Christmas DRESS
Just like Cinderella, where you had a GUESS,
Visiting you on your BIRTHDAY at your house, that DAY!
Was so SPECIAL because, as your 1st TEACHER…
there was no other WAY!

LEILAH

Mommy! Mommy! Look at me!
Flying like a butterfly and stinging like a bee.
My beautiful butterfly colors of: you KNOW!
I can jump high......and I can jump LOW!

STEVANIE

Activist Stevanie! Look at YOU!

From PRE-K to a YOUNG ADULT!,

you have GROWN with WINGS ...that's what you DO!

USE your VOICE! to make a DIFFERENCE in this WORLD TODAY!

You have a SUPPORTIVE father by your side, and I'm so PROUD of you,

No longer quiet! like RUBY BRIDGES your about to leave your MARK... HEY!

TANISHA

Ms Ruth! Ms Ruth! Look at ME!

From a PRESCHOOLER, with my pigtails... I was only...THREE!

I came in your class, and you taught me well,

NOW! Im all GROWN UP! going to college to SOAR!

To fulfill my FULL DESTINY, and leave childish things in EARLY CHILDHOOD... at the DOOR!

BRIANA

Briana, Briana! You KNOW who you ARE,
AUNTIE, calls you Dr Bre, because, I BELIEVE…you WILL go FAR
Far enough, to become a CHILDREN'S PEDIATRICIAN,
that's what you CHOOSE to DO,
I'm so PROUD of you, at HOW you've SOARED, and,
on your BIRTHDAY at MEDICAL school,
you are Dr Bre ….that's WHO! I BELIEVE you can FLY!
Auntie's in your corner! SOAR!

KAYLA

Kayla, my SPECIAL NEICE, I am writing a POEM for YOU,
You have EXCELLED throughout the years, and your AUNTIE, is PROUD of you... through and THROUGH.
From GRADUATION as a 1st GRADER... to a YOUNG ADULT age 19 NOW,
Look at you, in your RED GRADUATION GOWN, a POET also!... WOW!
TIME flies! and I don't even know HOW!
Keep SOARING high!
Love, Auntie!

Look at us NOW! From pre-k, Kindergarten, Elementary and Junior HIGH,

We all SOARED as Ms. Ruth ADVISED, and NOW, we can TOUCH the SKY!

Read those books, complete your math, go to the library and complete all your homework WELL.

It WILL all PAY off in the end, you'll see, and only TIME will TELL...

CONCLUSION

My GOALS/ PROSPECTIVE AIM, for this SPECIAL, WITTY ideas, CREATIVITY, POETIC book, is to allow CHILDREN/YOUNG ADULTS, to, NOT, allow any LIMITATIONS, that might occur, during their DEVELOPMENT in becoming their OWN person in LIFE!

We as ADULTS, must SUPPORT any CAREER AMBITION, they might have, as an INDEPENDENT CANDIDATE... for GREATNESS in their OWN right. Like a SEED BIRTHED within them, we must ENABLE it to GROW, PRODUCING BEATIFUL BRANCHES of a MULTIPLE FRUIT, NOT crushed, but it must FLOURISH, reaching its FULL POTENTIAL limit in Life... and SOAR! Like an EAGLE! My TEACHER opinion coming out, as a GREAT lesson plan!

Even during this PANDEMIC, there is absolutely NO EXCUSE that are CHILDREN/ YOUNG ADULTS cannot be READY... for our... ADULTS tomorrow! I know you will ENJOY this PRESENTATION of Ms Ruth's GENIUS PROJECT... outside of the CLASSROOM... where it all BEGAN!

WHERE is Ms Ruth NOW???

Right HERE! EXCELLING as an AUTHOR/ POET/ TEACHER...for TODAY!

THANK you my STUDENTS/ PARENTS for making this SPECIAL PROJECT *"finally take off"* like a rocket!

This is my BABY... I have NURTURED/ LOVED/INVEST in... do the SAME With your CHILD/ CHILDREN/ YOUNG ADULT...

Appreciate your SUPPORT! in 5 yrs from now, this HARD BACK cover will be a REMINDER... 1 GIFTED TEACHER... BELIEVED in my CHILD/ YOUNG ADULTS FUTURE ACCOMPLISHMENTS... because I had SOMEONE to BELIEVE in me! My MOTHER Bertha Mitchell, who is such a GREAT INSPIRATION to me, (my No 1 CHEERLEADER); Mrs MATTOS, my HAIRDRESSERS mom, who loves me like a DAUGHTER; my BEST FRIEND Carol, who is also my No 1 CHEERLEADER who NOURISHES me with her ENCOURAGEMENT; my 1st MENTOR when I ARRIVED in USA from LONDON ENGLAND, Zenifer Khan, a GRANDMOTHER figure, who saw GREATNESS in me, all those yrs ago and many more, as I am very POPULAR APPRECIATE you ALL!

From Ms Ruth, at age 5 ..she is now... an ENTREPRENEUR for GREATNESS! Yippee!

What ever you're called to do, DO YOUR BEST!!!

I would like to DEDICATE this SPECIAL MINI BIO, to my 2 NIECES, Kayla and Briana, who have BOTH EXCELLED Greatly throughout the years, and ACCOMPLISHING many GOALS of their CHOICE. Both SUCCESSFUL, in their OWN right.

I am very PROUD of them BOTH. Within this SPECIAL PROJECT of their ENGLISH Auntie, you will see, how BOTH of them has INSPIRED me, from their ELEMENTARY years... to NOW! YOUNG ADULT life.

I VISITED my SISTER in GA, where they LIVE when they were age 7-9 WOW!

WHERE ARE THEY NOW? At age 19/21 WOW! How TIME has flown by. I only have my 31 ALBUMS (old school) lol, and 60 pic FRAMES... to REMEMBER now. My DARLINGS...ENJOY! Your MINI BIO...and SOAR continually as AUNTIE taught you!

I love you much!

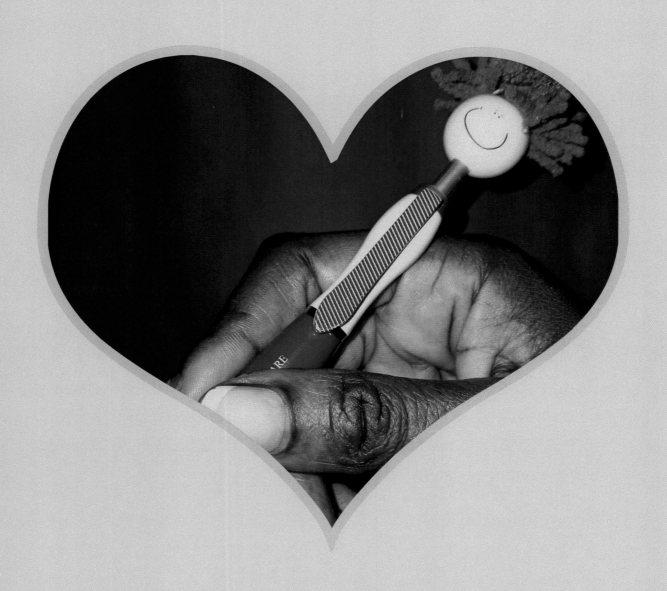

After the WRITING, there is TYPING. It's a process you KNOW…
HARD LABOR in ORGANIZATION, but the REWARD will be GREAT,
know that I told you SO,
My work is EASY, like a duck towards water that… FLOWS,
this was once in an INCABATER (so to speak).. NOW! RELEASED…
I can say to myself….'there it GOES!

The SPECIAL book was PRODUCED/ DELIVERED from my WOMB….(
so to speak) like a natral BABY…in 3 and a half months on 2-15-2021….
it was COMPLETED! Yippie! …ENJOY! As it's coming! …straight
from the ♥…INVESTING in all my ADORABLE STUDENTS from
PRESCHOOLERS….to YOUNG ADULTS! What Are They Called To
Be! ….PRINCE/ PRINCESS'S…for their GENERATION…of EXELLENCE!

Printed in the United States
by Baker & Taylor Publisher Services